Ambiguous Interpretations

my world.

MarQuetta "Shy Stilletto" Preston

AMBIGUOUS INTERPRETATIONS MY WORLD.

Copyright © 2021 by MarQuetta "Shy Stilletto" Preston.

All rights reserved. No part of this book may be reproduced or transmitted in any form or by any means without the written permission from the author or publisher.

Published by:
Ware Resources and Publishing
www.wareresources.com

1-888-469-4850 Ext. 2

ISBN 978-1-7360798-0-5
LCCN# 2020949507

Printed in USA by Ware Resources and Publishing

Acknowledgments

First and always giving thanks to God, for he is worthy and has kept me full of will and belief in myself when I didn't believe.

To my mother Wilma Frances Preston, thank you for making me the strong woman I am today and teaching me that one can truly make it alone. I thank God for assigning you to my life you are an earthly angel, I love you.

I would like to give a special thanks to Cho "Raymond" Woods. Thanks for making me believe in myself, and for the extra push you gave me to go after my dreams. In a world full of non-believers, the one person that believes in you makes all the difference. If I could thank you a million times it would never be enough, for you inspire me and always have supported my work. Thank you.

Thank you to all that believed in my creativity, and took the time to read all my first poetry works, being my audience/critics/readers you helped me to improve.

Finally, I'm thankful for all the relationships I had that failed, for they fueled most of these works. Thanks guys, for the wonderful learning experience of love and hurt.

Oh yeah, thanks for taking the time to read this page.

Dedication

I dedicate this book of poetry to those whom have ever dared to dream. Follow your dreams and whatever you want you shall have. Just free your mind from negativity and have faith in the true existence in which is you. Believe in yourself even if no one else believes in you, because you can make all things happen.......

To all my fellow poets...
Keep Poetry Alive!!!!!!!

You're about to witness the poetry works of Shy Stilletto a.k.a. MarQuetta Jeanelle Preston all original no samples. Some of the content, language, and / or poetry may not appeal to you at all, but I would like to thank you for taking the time to read this body of work. No I'm not a Spoken Word Poet, however I am a poet nonetheless. I write so others may read and apply their own reality to my rhyme and thoughts. Please take this time to open your mind, feel, read, and enjoy these words from my mind to your ears, mind, heart and soul. Enjoy...

A Brief Description of Me

A massive lover of harmonized beauty and order. A wise giver of all that is beautiful, different and new. I can sort out the good from the bad; cutting through the bull is my inherited tool. Independent to the fullest and by God above I'm blessed. All these traits are found in me and me only, for this is just a brief description of me.

Ambiguous- (am-big'u-us) - Susceptible of multiple interpretations.

Interpretation (s) - (inter'pret-a"shon (s)) - A concept of a work of art as expressed by the writer, character and style of its representation or performance.

Contents

Acknowledgments ... v
Dedication ... vii
A Brief Description of Me ... xi
Again... ... 1
All About Me... ... 2
Allow the Persuasion... ... 3
But Still... ... 4
Can You Handle It... ... 5
Chance Meeting... ... 6
Comfortable Entanglement... ... 7
Damn What About Me... ... 8
De-Energized... ... 9
Drink Me... ... 11
Dropping Science of the Heart ... 12
Eclipse of the Sun... ... 14
Emotionless Mask... ... 15
Empty... ... 16
For A Rose Is Still A Rose... ... 17
Friendly Physical Connection... ... 18
Heavenly Purgatorial Hellish Experience... ... 19
Hurt... ... 21
I Couldn't Say It... ... 22
I Got You... ... 24
I Said all this to say.... ... 25
I Wished for You... ... 26
I'm Not Her... ... 27
Insist... ... 28
Jazzy Gentleman ... 29

Just Once.	30
Let Me Go...	31
Lonely Thoughts..	32
Love and Respect.	33
Mask of True Emotion	34
My Friends Secret Admiration.	35
Player..	36
Please Don't Bring Me Your Funny Money Blues..	37
Positively Twenty-One.	38
Predictable...	39
Prelude of a First Kiss.	40
Promising Threat of a Plus Sized Diva (The Show Is Mine)..	41
Re- Birth.	42
Remembering.	43
Remembering Love.	44
Running...	45
Salt in My Wounds.	47
Self-Discovery..	49
Shadow..	50
So Here I Sit.	51
Thank You.	52
Thoughts of Desperation.	53
Thug Angel.	54
Trapped.	55
Wasteland.	56
What a Sweet Ride.	58

Again

I'm sitting here upset again, because of things I allowed you to get away with. My stress isn't your fault, but a fault of my own because I allowed you to walk all over me.

Doing whatever it took to please you and neglecting my wants, my needs and myself. Holding on to lost dreams of us that will never exist, I know this but refuse to accept it.

You're all I see, and you know this so you continue to blind me with your lies. Hurting me and not caring how I feel. But I can't blame you because I allowed this to happen again.

It's obvious you're hiding lots of things from me; like it's obvious I found you out, but I'm afraid to say I've done so because I love you.

Although love shouldn't hurt I keep taking the punches you hurl at me. My brain not registering that my heart can't take any more pain produced by you.

Again I'm losing the game. Again I'm feeling pain. Again the love I need is the love that doesn't want me. Again I'm crying tasting the salt of my own tears; with no one to console me, or hold me where I lay. Again I've been played by the game.

All About Me

Full of passion, fire and desire; to be with you is what I aspire.
Each meeting session sets my heart a fire; her having you I admire.

My admiration's sometimes get the best of me, but are blinded by her stupidity, because she hasn't a clue about you loving me.

Furious is what she would be if she knew that every time you kissed her you're thinking of me.
Playing with my emotions too probably, but I won't let silly shit like that stop me. For pursuing you is what I choose to do, and I won't stop until I have you.

I know you think I'm touched and sometimes wonder why I love you so much. I won't give up for the life of me, I want you and it's all about me.

Allow the Persuasion

Allow me to memorize you with the influence of my lips, drunken you with the taste of my cocoa lips; full, succulent and intoxicating.

Allow me to set your mind a journey when I beckon you with my brunette eyes. Persuasively hypnotizing you with sweltering dreams of pinkness.

Allow me to lead you to a canopy of rainbows. Where shadows reflect gold walls dripped with silver that predict hope and give birth to new horizons of pleasure. Channeling you to the canal where new life begins, and P- funk and blue notes sing on high.

Allow me to take you to that place full of sensual emotions and contentment; that guarantee satisfaction and warm blissful delight.

Allow me to take you to that next level; where you never thought you'd go. Relaxing your ego, gripping your intellect, making you wonder what's next.

Allow me to expedition through your cranium and whisper to your thoughts. Telling secrets of how deep I really can be. Starting mind gossip about you belonging to me.

Allow me to auction this pink persuasion to you, making a love possession transaction brought out by you. Allow the persuasion.

But Still

I've reminisced a million times, yet the outcome has never changed. Although I wished it would have many times, and for this reason you remain special to me. When I saw you for the first time in a long time, it was like seeing you for the first time all over again. Looking at you; your lips called out to me and your body spoke to me. I tried to hold back the want to kiss your lips and caress your needing body, for the flashbacks were all too familiar. Up until this point I never knew I missed or felt for you this much. Finally speaking your mouth said all the things my mind was thinking, and once again I was lost in you.

Afraid we never took our friendship to the next level for we have too much to lose if things didn't work as planned. All the while you were what I needed, and I was what you needed, but we just didn't know it and still don't know it.

Taunting me you ask "What I want?" Knowing it's you, yet you want to hear it so you can reject me again. So what's your point, your angle, your game?

Regretfully I can't turn back time to show you, nor can I move forward in you, for besides the friendship the rest of this relationship is a game to you.

But still I love you.

Can You Handle It

Put up or shut up is the key phrase. Running off at the mouth seems to be the only thing men do these days. Playing the game some never win, before I choose a lover I'd rather have a friend.

I'm lonely it's true, still that doesn't mean I want to rush things with you. A little time is not much to ask, I'd rather know you fully before loving you becomes a task... I've had many heartaches although in my past, so are you sure you could love me completely is what I ask. No I'm not judging or comparing you, not one bit. I'm just one to test the water before jumping head first into it. Now if you think you can handle all the above let's begin work on a strong foundation that will hold our house of love.

Chance Meeting

A gazing feeling interrupts me. My mind nor body prepared for what my eyes were about to see.

With one quick glance you sexually intoxicate me, and with each word spoken you mentally intrigue me. Now intertwined in your suave seduction I see things I wouldn't normally, but yet to wonder what someone like you would see in someone like me. Pinch me; my mind is screaming, chance meetings like this don't happen to me often so I must be dreaming. My eyes are seeing someone so vivid and sensual, I wonder was this a chance meeting or intentional.

Comfortable Entanglement

I made the mistake of understanding you incorrectly. Placing me in a cozy position you confused me. Made me tense, yet you expected me to relax. Although your intrigue was soothing I knew I would never have you completely to myself. Jealously I possessed you placing you in this warm lonely place in my heart; protecting you, never giving you the ability to tarnish or allowing you to flee. See I got use to you softly massaging me when we emerged in sensual contact. Comfortably meshing with you is all I wanted to do. Maybe I misunderstood when you said you loved me, maybe what you meant was you loved using me. See you've got me so deeply involved in this love affair that it has become comfortably embarrassing to me, and I can't free myself. Tell me how can someone that touches me so soft, with looks of positive outcome be so selfish? You thought only of yourself when you made this love arrangement, now I'm all caught up with you in this comfortable entanglement.

Damn What About Me

12:30 am, 1:00 am or 3:45; you leave my thighs without looking into my eyes. You rush to dress and like a sweep of brutal winter air you're gone again. Leaving me to soak up our love juices and too lay alone on saturated sheets.

Rushing, rushing, rushing you go home and for a few hours in her embrace you forget all about me. Making love to her I'm completely erased from your mind.

You keep rushing, rushing until your rushing catches up with you, and when she finds out about me what will you do?

You'll remove me from your mind for all eternity, leaving me to wonder damn what about me.

De-Energized

De-energized; It's a word in my mental dictionary meaning all that is you has been sucked and blown away to a breezeless sky held in anxiety forever, never regaining motion or returning. You're stuck, that rock and hard place won't budge; losing it quickly you experience a mental shut down seeing nothing but storm clouds and darkness.

How many times have you died?

Me; I've died about a million times, only to keep on living. Only to continue to hate myself. Only to continue to hate the people around me. How many times have you loved? Me; I've love six million times, only to be hurt by it. Only to continue to try to love again. Why is it that we try so hard to love people that don't love us back? Why is that we try to fit into the spectrum which others think is the right size, shape, or color. You don't know? Will let me tell you what I think. It's the want that drives you. That want to be loved, desired, cared about, beautiful, to just have all your positive energy reflected back on you. Here's something freaky for you though; there is no such thing as love, dying, or a spectrum to fit in. Unless you're fitting in your own spectrum, loving yourself, and letting that view that others have of you die. Survive no matter what; do what you got to do to be you, forget everything and everybody else.

Answer this; if you were to have a next to death experience and lost all things that you took for granted like your sight, smell, touch, movement and money. Would you survive off of love, would those people in the spectrum come to your aid? Are you thinking, have you thought? Time's up; let me answer. You would probably die. See you don't know love because it was always given to you emotionlessly, with consequences, or it just wasn't available. That spectrum you thought you'd fit in had already thrown you out, and you failed to realize that you have been, had been and always will be dead for you never lived for you, or loved yourself. Holding up that smile and that fake ass person you called you had worn you out. Pushed you to the edge and you broke, and there was no one there to break your fall.

Falling off of that never ending plane in which you thought was a solid surface. When things got too heavy it crumbled, leaving you covered in rubble and grief. Leaving you to energize yourself, pull yourself out, breathe again, to live and let die. Left for dead in this world of obscure devotion and fake acts of kindness, yet you have a strong desire to keep on loving and caring for the same people that will never care for, or love you. The final question is will you survive, or will you be de-energize?

Drink Me

If I could convert my heart into a liquid state; I would fill your glass 'til it overflowed, so you could taste my love. Intoxicating you with my fire water I state claim on your lips so you'll never crave another. Making you full I'll encourage you to keep drinking me.

Drink me.

Allow me to dissolve deeper and deeper into you, making you react only to me. Like liquor I'm that pure grain let me get you high. Liquefied in you; flowing through your veins so I know your feeling me. Making my way to your brain so you'll never forget me.

Drink me.

Let me melt away the myths about love you've heard before; drink me, for I'm that liquefied addiction that will leave you wanting more.

Drink me.

Dropping Science of the Heart

Big arms, back of steel, voice smooth as silk with massive sex appeal. Damn you're immeasurable in a scientific type of way, you're vast in my mind every minute, second and hour of the day. In a crowd of millions you didn't go unnoticed, from the moment I saw you I kept you in my focus. You're methodical and I; I'm your understudy. Watching your every move learning your craft, and praying one day you'll love me.

My tunnel vision channeled in on you, the world stopped as if no one else existed but me and you. Damn you're meticulous and I'm impressed with the careful way you caress me without knowing your doing so, I'm wide open feeling your energy and I don't plan to let go.

Your eyes exotic, physical bionic, energy cosmic and if I can't have you it will be tragic. My thoughts now erotic letting me know it's time to work some magic. Although fate and destiny maybe playing a part your biology and chemistry sparked a chain reaction in my heart. Damn you're the bomb dropping science and dissecting my heart and mind scrupulous, cutting deep and precise each and every time. My thoughts tripping over my tongue, mind clouded with lust and love. Lips trembling praying for help from above.

My lips finally spoke hello as I looked in your eyes, my mind went crazy chanting the words my my my. You've got every part of me colliding with confusion over you, my mind in a panicking frenzy and the results could be combustible. Damn you're nuclear, your cause and effect is dangerously hazardous. So here I am thinking up an equation which would make you + me = us.

You've got my heart dropping science, because I can't figure out if this is fate, destiny or love.

Eclipse of the Sun

Dark now my vision has eclipse all view of you. Thick sheets of darkness now obstruct where I would only see you. Beautiful things I used to see are in focus now and ugly. I truly felt you were the one for me. You were my light shined through what ever had a hold on me, I have you no more how can this be. I wanted to love you placing you with the Gods and the sun, making a bond of love that couldn't be broken by anyone. Tricking me, leaving me wondering "What did I do?" Now that the smoke has cleared I see I've done nothing, just tried to love you. Remember the old saying that goes "Let love go and it will come back to you." Well in the state of mind I'm in I say fuck you and love too. Kicking myself daily because I thought you were the one when all along you were just another mother fucker totally eclipsing my sun.

Emotionless Mask

Telling you I love you, I receive no response from you. Distant like an enormous landscape I can't grasp all of you. Calling your name my heart overflowing with tears, losing you is what I fear. Crying out everyone but you can hear. A steel wall placed before me, I admit you're really hurting me. Eyes of stone holding back how you really feel for me. Going through all these changes with you is making me crazy.

Sick of you toying with my emotions that are real. Tables have turned now, so how does it feel? Drained now, no more games will be played, this is the end and we can't be friends. Yes I see your tears, but how about the ones I cried for so many years. Did you ever stop to realize what you did to me, or consider showing me a little sympathy? Stop no need; I can answer that for you. You did me so wrong but yet I still adored you. Work things out? No thanks I'll pass. Hard was the task of loving your tired ass, so now in place of my heart is an emotionless mask.

Empty

At this point I'm containing nothing, holding no occupants.

Shamelessly I can admit; I'm empty and not another love song will play in my heart, for love don't live here anymore.

So many have mistaken lust as love to the point where I can't tell a break up from abandonment. Left open, heart yearning for attention and it hurts.

It's funny how hurt can exist where love should live. Like it's funny that I've tried to love and love again only to be slapped in the face by humiliation over and over again.

My sole is echoing and the hollow walls of my heart are screaming.

I've emptied my heart of love for others to learn to live +for myself. Yes I want to feel and love deeply, but I can't because I'm empty.

For A Rose Is Still A Rose

Hey love I'm sending a bouquet of black roses to you; hopefully all the tattered pieces of your heart have mend, and the blood has soaked up too.

The love I once had for you was so strong, I often wonder what went wrong. Our love affair ended in a rapid halt and I always blamed myself, although it wasn't my fault. You never apologized for all the lies and deceit, so I thought black roses how sweet.

Afraid; why should you be, you should've been afraid before when you did all you did to me. All I wanted was an apology and you refused. So now life or death you must choose. Fed up, deaf to your threats. I'm about to take your life, hasn't that registered yet? Obviously not, because your still talking. Don't turn your back on me or you'll be a dead man walking.

What goes around comes around and I've warned you too many times, so say good bye and don't try to change my mind.

Ugly were the things you've done to me, hopefully God will forgive me when I show up in all black to deliver these black roses as your family gives your eulogy.

Friendly Physical Connection

"What we have is physical" fell from those lips I looked forward to kissing and they stung, because I thought we had a special friendship.

Looking back I can remember getting caught up, lost deep in the thought of us and the sensual scenes we would create and how you would leave me longing for more.

The connection we made could not be measured to any I've had before. You touched me in places that longed for a masculine caress. Awakening parts of me I wasn't aware of and I thank you, yet looking back I know our connection was a major physical mistake.

The stigmas of your words continue to simmer and will forever be branded in my head. For you allowed your fear of loving me to speak for you.

Respecting you and your views of our friendship I said nothing just listened to you; my friend tell me I meant nothing and our connection was one of physical nature when we both knew it was much more.

Afraid to give up your heart again you felt the need to re-remind me that you were not and would never be mine. Knowing this was our pact from the start made things worse, for I thought our friendship was much more than a friendly physical connection.

Heavenly Purgatorial Hellish Experience

Your name's loudly amplified in my head and I can't stop thinking about you. Emotional, each tear drop brought on by you. I'm in a serious purgatorial state; punishing myself for the personal sin, no mistake of letting myself go too fast and loving you too soon. Suffering more and more every time I think of your touch; no you. Feelings of great sickness envelope me, reminding me of love longed for but could never be. How dare you put this whammy on me tricking me into believing you actually cared for me?

Your intent was pure selfishness with a dab of evil, you hypnotized and mesmerized me with the skill of the devil. How did you do it? Easing yourself in my heart, my head and my bed. Feeding me lies when it should have been the fruit of truth instead. How dare you deceive me; got me crying real tears over you, turning my enormous beautiful blue skies into ones that are itty bitty gray and miserable.

You were my angel. I only saw heaven and halos when I looked at you, with a glorified aura although hell festered inside of you.

Fallen fast from my grace, now I can't stand your touch, voice or your face. Blazing with what I thought was a heavenly glow how I to know you, my angel had horns and were in fact the devil.

Selfless I gave to you, handled myself in a disregardful manner just to make sure you were comfortable. Double-crossed you crossed me out of all future plans with you.

I often dreamt of swimming in the beautiful tropical turquoise seas, showering you with my summer rain of love to show you how much

I cared and loved you, this just leaves three things to be true. I was in heaven the first time I met you. When you left with no explanation purgatory took over the situation. Pure hell is what I feel with every thought of you. Now I'd like to thank you for a heavenly purgatorial hellish experience you made come true. Thank you

Hurt

I've been trying to let the love I have for you die and act as if it never lived. Packing it away in the deepest depths of my heart I keep it a secret, never whispering a word of it to you ever again. Like currency I continued to give you all the love I had, with hopes of owning your heart. Now I see I made a bad investment, which may take me years to recover from. I'm broke and I'm not sure how I'm going to fix things. You were my dramatic fiction and I fantasized of living happily ever after with you, but it was just my imagination running away with me and I've lost the ability to confront and deal with reality by using the creative powers of my mind. And this is all too real to me. Why did you have to treat my love so slanderous? Causing injury to my wellbeing, making a lie out of the notable beauty of our love. You chose to leave this chorus singing love songs on high, to dance to the beat of many different drummers. Now I'm solo, an individual voice crying the blues over loving you.

I Couldn't Say It

My thoughts got all caught up; causing my lips to remain silent, so the truth of my heart would not fall from them. Gripping my words my mind screamed "Tell him!", but I couldn't say it.

Musing over the things, I planned to tell you if ever giving the chance again; yet I still couldn't tell you how much I felt for you when I knew you before, or how I thought of you when we lost touch for too many years. I couldn't tell you how I really felt when we found each other again. When I saw you for the first time in a long time, I was reminded of how I've longed for you. Finally I found my friend with whom I lost on good terms. Our re-connection was all so familiar and from the first hug I felt firmly attached again. I wanted to scream I love you and tell you how much I missed you, but with the thought of how risqué that would've been I held back. Now contemplating on things I should've told you up-front how I felt then, but I Couldn't say it.

Fighting my emotions and the fact that I desire you actively I try to act like having a friendship with benefits is okay when in fact I cherish you and my adoration makes me want more.

Now that beneficial reasoning has taken place I can now see the profitable acquaintance I've made in you. I also know that in relationships based on lust there's no such thing as devotion, faithfulness, affection or real adoration so you and I both lose. However, in relationships based on love, fondness and true emotion you always win. That's why I find it hard to look at you. Along with my want to be with you seriously, yet I love to look at you for those same reasons. When you're around, I try to take in your touch, smell, smile and the shape of your face so I'll never lose you again.

Often I find myself thinking of how it would've been if we never lost touch. I sometimes wonder what it would've been like to love you completely. I know you have someone yet I keep pushing to keep you close to me. It's not that I don't care about her feelings, but I'm just trying to keep that feeling I have when I'm around you.

While in your embrace I wanted to tell you all these things, but I couldn't say it due to fear of losing my friend.

I couldn't say it . . .

I Got You

You have a woman and yes I have a man, still it doesn't stop me from having you because I can. When she gets mad it makes me blush, because she doesn't know the half about us.

When he and I make love I call out his name, knowing damn well I'm thinking about you but hell its part of the game. When we make love and you ask "whose is it baby?" I slyly smile and answer "Yours maybe."

Now all this love could make an average sista sick, but I'm a true diva and I can handle it. Go ahead, let them say what they want to say. It's all in the game and everybody can't play.

A lot of love is what I have to give, but you must except and understand that my heart is half yours and half his. They say you can't have your cake and eat it too, I guess they were wrong because I got him and you too.

I Said all this to say . . .

Honesty marked by or displaying truthfulness and integrity, not deceptive or fraudulent. Honesty is pure sincerity.

Knowing myself all too well I've come to the realization that I'm falling in love with you. I don't expect you to feel the same, yet I can't pretend my feelings don't exist. Honestly from the start of our meeting I thought of no one but you. Yes, I have met other people however I have no interest in them because my thoughts overflow with you.

Maybe my heart is moving too fast, because I know we're just friends. Special friends, but friends no less. I guess your heart believes what it wants even when your mind knows the real deal. Funny right?

I've said all this to say I'm falling in love with you, but I respect you enough to leave the physical aspect of this relationship alone and just be extremely great platonic friends. This way I can shield my heart from the burn of disappointment.

I said all this to say . . .

What color negligee should I be wearing when you get here? lol

I Wished for You

Charming baritone voice of velvet, sweet, deep, dark, chocolate melanin dipped towering range of sexy refined manhood mania elegance. The brief description of your physical brings to mind a stimulating visual giving me more reasons to want you.

Astoundingly you've took over my mind set giving me nostalgic feelings as if before we've met. The first glance overwhelmed me it's true, I saw heaven in your eyes and an angel in you. Caught up in your seductive rapture thoughts existing only of you, lost in a world of sensual day dreams that can only be fulfilled by you.

In a trance, I'm mesmerized by the voodoo that you do so well; I wished for you. Now you've got me under your spell.

I'm Not Her

You've prolonged your existence in my life for far too long, and I must rid myself of you.

With a contorted heart you expect me to bend and cater to you with no question. You got me to the point where I'm asking myself how is it that you continue to pull me into your insecure world, playing the mother role. Having me make up for the lack of love you were given as a child.

Why is it that you punish me for your mother's mistakes as a woman, beating me down because she never hugged you or kissed you assuring you that things would be okay?

I've apologized for all the hurt that she caused you, so what more do I have to do to prove that I love you?

You've prolonged your existence in my life for far too long, and I must rid myself of you. I was your lover not your mother. I'm sorry she never shared her love with you, yet I'm the one you choose to make suffer. That's why we're through.

Insist

You insist on breaking me; making me feel worthless in your eyes, having obscured vision when it comes to me. Seeing nothing.

You insist on whispering sweet meaningless nothings; with deaf ears, when I talk, you hear nothing. Perceiving no sound.

You insist on engaging in the acts of deception; telling untruths about your love for me, with a black heart protected by hatred. When I try to express love to you, you reject it. Reacting to nothing.

You insist on kissing me as if I were a stranger; pretending you're not obligated. Passionately I try to spark a flame. Overpoweringly you pull away. Feeling nothing.

You insist on controlling your caress; fighting the familiar embrace that we once shared. Insultingly pulling away. Suffering I try to clinch onto you but my grasp isn't strong enough to keep you, you criticize it. Caring about nothing.

Enduring this fabricated experience I'm finally seeing the real you for the first time. I now perceive all your wicked sounds; the misleading words that once sounded so beautiful. I'm now reacting to your fictitious actions, with a heart of stone. Feeling strong now I know I can overcome you. Through with your forged caring and insulting reactions to my actions I insist this obscure devotion end.

Jazzy Gentleman

Every essence of you is full of different textures and sounds, beautiful like jazz steadfast, yet soft and easy. The way you look at me, I can tell you see me like no other has seen me.

Your feelings are so hard and strong like the sound of an alto saxophone, but your expression's rolls off your lips relaxed as one of a soprano make. You have the ability to get deep with my depth. A jazzy gentleman, standing strong where others would have left.

I get lost just thinking of you, with wishes of a dark, sensual, rhythmic harmonized sunsets, giving birth to melodic percussion filled sunrises I pray will come true.

I dream of you Mr. Jazzy; you're music, music not even Coltrane could write. Even if I can't have you here in the flesh at sunrise; at least I'll have you in my dreams when the sunsets at night.

Just Once

Having beauty in any of its forms is said to be pleasing to the senses or the mind; yet I'm benighted by my own reflection, wondering what's wrong with me and when would someone find my beauty.

Overtaken by self-doubt as if it were darkness I mentally battle myself trying to see the brighter picture but I can't.

I've heard somewhere that loveliness pertains to that which inspires ardent emotion rather than intellectual appreciation; which would explain why I attract dumb mother fuckers, yet these same mother fuckers claim to feel me.

Just once I would like to be extremely desirous.

Just once I want to experience the success of loving.

Just once I want to feel the happiness of wanting what I get and not settling for a man I can't stand to look at or cringe at the thought of him making love to me.

Just once I want to feel passion filled touch and not feel like I'm being violated.

Just once I want to be pleasing to the senses and the mind claiming my own beauty.

Just once I want to be lovely, touched passionately and love completely... just once.

Let Me Go

I'm trying to make sense of the nonsense you've put me through, trying to make sense of the fact that I'm in love with you. But I can't. Although you're gone and out my life completely my mind keeps playing games making me think you need me. You're haunting me. You're here and I can still feel you, the more I feel the more I hate you. Some days your presence is much stronger, I have to remind myself your on this earth no longer. You surround me. My mind is overloaded with all the years, memories and tears I've cried for you, my heart is full yet I'm lonely and I can't make room to love because I still love you. You're a ghost and I feel your presence around me, now I ask that you let me go so I can love freely.

Love and Respect

You asked if I loved you. If I said no how would you feel? Love is a strong word full of emotions that are real. First loving your mind then your body and soul. Making sure the love I have for you is expressed as a whole.

Now I could lie to you and make up all sorts of stuff, but would these words be enough to make you see that I care for you, will always be there for you, would sacrifice for you, would even give my life for you.

The actions that I show could never be put into just one phrase, so the answer is I respect you a lot and I'll love you some day. See love isn't something one plans to do. Love isn't something you seek, but it finds you. To have you in my world, I'd do anything its true. But it wouldn't be worth it if I didn't receive love and respect from you.

Mask of True Emotion

Never allowing fear to show on my face; for I will not allow fear to live in my heart, so I fear not.

Never allowing hurt to show on my face; for I will not allow hurt to live in my soul, which makes me stronger.

Never allowing defeat to live in my mind, so I'll always be a winner.

Happiness is the only emotion I'll allow to show on my face, so that makes me a liar.

True happiness comes from being true to self... When will I start to be honest?

My Friends Secret Admiration

I have a friend with a keen interest in you. She's so intrigued she finds excitement in everything you do. Her nerves gather at the pit of her stomach each time she sees you, it's true. So I've been sent to deliver these few words to you.

I was told to tell you how she really likes, thinks of you at night, how you send her mind and emotions on flights . . . Well maybe I'm exaggerating a little for you, but trust my friend really has it bad for you.

Player

In order to deal with you my mind set has to be on a win or take all basis, for I know the outcome may be uncertain. See I already know loving you will be a gamble, but I've decided to try my luck. Willing to take on the challenges I set high stakes, submerging into you. Knowing more than likely that wages of loving you would be hurt, but I plan to roll the dice anyway. From the first time I saw you I was willing to surrender all and take a risk on you, sacrificing everything I placed all bets on you. See I don't plan to give up on this venture, because you will be my fortune. Placing my heart on the table with hopes of gaining a lover and friend. Playing your game I'm not about to forfeit and lose; I'm feeling lucky knowing I would be the champion if my victory were you, so I'm playing to win.

Ambiguous Interpretations

Please Don't Bring Me Your Funny Money Blues

Ready to party; broke as hell, looking like a million bucks. Paying to get your hair done, but can't by food and such.

Lights flickering, cable fuzzing, car payment due and your landlord's bugging. Kids put out of daycare for two weeks, won't pay for sanitation so the garbage is starting to stink.

Your nails need filling and you want a new pair of shoes, but the phone's about to be cut off so which will you choose?

Pay check to pay check living is really taking its toll, and all of your broken promises to the bill collectors are getting old.

You could work like I do and save for a rainy day, but you rather run around buying up all the Gucci and Hennessy.

Bill collectors sending you those "Don't let me catch your ass in the street." notices. So caught up with bling bling mentality you've lost focus.

So please don't come to me crying you're broke, because I'm sick and tired of your funny money blues and that's no joke.

Positively Twenty-One

Of all days why did today have to be the day my life decided to alter so drastically, and ever so completely? No, I haven't been the best at everything, nor am I the worst; however not in a million years would I have ever thought this would be my punishment for wanting a better life. Shit I'm only twenty-one years old, with the world at my grasp. Now I'm losing touch with everything. My world is full of darkness no color, just a black sky with no air to be breathed in or exhaled out. My once bright eyes are now dark and dim, and I'm losing sight of all that is positive except for my results.

Sitting here in a daze, my mind took me to a world with antiseptic filled wind streams, and clouds that look like white lab coats, and the only thing I can hear is the sun whispering "You're Positive." Snapped back to reality I tell myself "You're going to live," but in my dream world the birds chirp "You're going to die." Deep right, but that's how far I got to dig to pull myself out of this rut and live again, while my blood stream is dying, along with my dreams of a long life of happiness.

See where I'm from scholarships are produced from the motions in your hips, and young girls are always being scouted, and placed on the Dean's List. I hoed for my clothes, let my looks pay for my books, and when the old heads wanted to cop some feel I got free meals. No I'm not happy but I had to do what I had to survive to make my life better, nevertheless it's even worse now.

Fading in and out of my day dream I hear an educated man saying things like treatment drugs, prolonging life, protection, and living a normal life. Living a normal life that has never been me, and will never be, for I'm positive and twenty-one, twenty-one positively.

Predictable

You're not unpredictable; you're multi-dimensional, with all sorts of things hidden in your darkness. But like a ray of light I see through your secrets, lies, broken assurance and fake guarantees. You stepped into my place call perfect soiling it with deception, but I knew you would. When I first caught glimpse of your eyes, I predicted you would hurt me. Excusing your ploy, I went along with the humdrum full of stupidity. I predicted you would sweep through my mind set like an air stream causing me mind numbing pain, jolting up dust from past relationships. Having me doing strenuous things I swore I'd never do for love again, reverting back to the filth of stupidity. I predicted your eyes were telling a whole other story from what I'm reading now, but never thought hurt and duplicity could be so tedious or written so pretty. I was sightless as your eyes spoke free verses of sensual togetherness and long term relations, but like a good novel you pulled me into a fantasy world of trickery. You're not unpredictable you're a thief, stealing my thoughts replacing them with sole vision of you. Hypnotized I gave all of me. Hurt now because I allowed you to be so predictable of me.

Prelude of a First Kiss

Conversation interesting, but left at a minimum. I try to stray away from your eyes and the passion in them. I feel you looking into my soul deep within me, bringing out all the shyness hidden inside of me. Your body language speaking in a tongue I much understand, you're weakening me with each touch of your hand. Trembling excited by temptation wanting to feel your body and experience your sweet sensation. The first kiss started it all; sweet and succulent, feeling the soft textures of your lips there my mind went. Soaring high into wonderland with passion filled dreams that can only be fulfilled by one and you're that man. Raising me to another level. I've never experienced anything like this, you amazingly mesmerized me and it only took one kiss. God; please don't let this end was my silent prayer, ready for a sensual voyage to Atlantis and only you can take me there. Your sexual aggression rough yet arousing, the way you caress me trying to see how far I'll let you go. You're really testing me.

We interlude into the act. You're irresistible and I can't resist you. I've dreamed of a moment like this before, now what I've dreamt has finally come true. I'm in a state of pure bedazzlement, you're holding and thrusting me with love. I'm feeling your vibrant thing and thanking the Gods above. Could you be the king that'll chase away my sorrow? I hope so, now that I have you in my clutches I don't plan or want to let go. Claiming you; I leave a lover's signature of scratches on your strong back. Never to share with another was our sensual pact. This brings on the end of our composition, the conclusion of the act. Infatuation made way for fornication. I can't believe this or how it all reflected from the prelude of a first kiss.

Promising Threat of a Plus Sized Diva (The Show Is Mine)

A Diva from the day I touch the earth. Standing tall and strong ready to claim my turf. I won't stand for your discrimination or negativity for they are results of your jealousy.

Standard? No that's never been me. On a scale of one to ten I'm a ninety. It took a long time to build my self-esteem you see and that I have it you can't touch me.

I'm not your usual standard damn it! With moo moos and sheets for clothing, these are contour fashion designs I'm wearing; along with a designer bag I'm holding.

Yes I'm a Queen sized lady sporting a double D happily, and upon entering a room all eyes are on me constantly.

You said it couldn't be done, so I had to do it. Buy a ticket to the show so you'll be witness to it. Better yet buy a VIP front row seat, so you can see me up close making my debut looking so sweet.

Picture it; Showtime hips swinging, lights flashing me the big girl in the midst of all the action. Strutting down the runway, you see me. Sitting there all mad because you can't be me. Oops better get up quickly cause I'm the Queen and it's time you hail to me.

This is a promising threat from me to you, so until next time I'm done and my statement is through.

Re-Birth

Covering up what I really feel inside. Me the person I am I always seem to hide. Never truly happy with what I see in me, always thinking of better things that could become of me. Wishing I was some else at any cost, with thoughts like this I know my soul will be lost. I wear many hats with many talents and capabilities, but when I need support it seems like no one's there for me.

Told I was a black Queen that could accomplish all my dreams. Those who told me self-worth was all that mattered are the same those whom sharp tongues helped my dreams shatter.

Good enough one minute, but not the next. I feel all my dreams have been hexed. Hating myself I never considered my self-worth, I guess I never will until I give re-birth.

Remembering

Your scent lingers eons after you depart. I can still see your shadow in the candle lit ambiance I so lovingly created, I still see your footprints in the flower petal love trail that led to my embrace. I still remember the oil, wax, lace and the look of appreciation on your face. For you never experienced anything like this.

Although you never uttered a word your facial expression and reaction told a thousand stories, recited a million poems and sang a billion love songs. All that needed to be said was said, but in a language and tone only I could hear and we understood. Secretly we set the standards for our love traditions, gracefully inviting new and exciting ideals. Keeping open minds for we never knew what the other was thinking.

Blindfolded with candlelight and kisses we led one another to different mind sets fulfilling all our wishes. Still, we spoke not one word. Our silence was the only statement of approval needed to be heard.

Glistening with perspiration and smiles we traveled and explored each other to no end. I remember soothing and massaging your mind, body, and ego. Held in a tight embrace; I never wanted to let you go. Holding on to every second like our last; the hours passed by slowly. Exchanging intense looks; concentrated gawking turns into scandalous, passionate, dramatic bliss. I name you Champion Lover for no one has ever made me feel like this.

Remembering Love

When loneliness begins to set in; I think of you and the love we use to be in. I think of all the love that was built, and once more my dreams are fulfilled.

But from guilt I pinch myself for recalling you and all the things we use to do. Knowing how hard it was, but oh well I'm just remembering love.

Running

My mind constantly running since I started running for my life. Even when I'm quiet I'm constantly thinking, praying, begging, hoping and apologizing for things I've done in and to my life.
Praying that I haven't destroyed all possibilities of family and love.

Begging for forgiveness hoping I'm forever healthy, able to have children and watch them grow. Hoping I'll find love and keep a man and grow old with him.

Apologizing to myself for the stress, self-hatred, wear, tear and the hollow walls of empty I've built.

Running, reality steady sinking in and the fact that I wasn't always 100% protected in my sexual situations have set in and I'm afraid. Praying to God to please protect me, for I don't want to die young or be a casualty of my senseless actions.

Running looking for that feeling said to animate a person who is genuinely fond of someone . . . Love, yet I keep running into the feeling marked by strong attachment to foolish unreasonable love or desire . . . Lust.

I'm lost and rundown, yet my mind is constantly running, thinking and longing for that which is an ardent bond of loyal affection.

Running looking and searching for devoted attachment. Learning to distinguish the deference between love and lust; finding the ability to love myself completely.

I'm tired of apologizing, begging, hoping, longing, looking and thinking; yet I pray for the strength to keep running until I'm free. I have to keep running to be completely free. I have to keep running to be completely me.

Salt in My Wounds

Killing me softly; internally torn I swore to never trust another mother fucker like you, but I thought you were different.

I silence myself for the words I want to spit at you would puncture your mind set and be as poisonous as venom.

I sit trying to figure out what could have provoked this, but nothing makes sense, yet the salt of your betrayal and disrespect has soaked in and it stings.

Your appearance was completely fraudulent and your true intent was pure deception. Deceiving me making me think I had a true friend in you.

Efficient; you made sure you injured my feelings, packing salt in my already pierced skin. Proving my sense of non- trust in you was correct.

I opened myself up to you showing you a new view of life, yourself and the possibilities of all positive things not knowing you were capable of cutting me so deeply.

Damn friend why did you have to season things. Tarnishing my image of you and to add more insult to injury you continue to smile in my face acting like nothing ever happened.

Unable to continue to put up with your counterfeit grins and fictitious laughter. I must break away forcefully from this friendship I thought would've never been severable. Cutting you off is a must for I have to appease myself, for I'm not fake. I can no longer pacify you or your feelings. But I'm wrong; right.

You re-created this incident into a drama-filled scene where you're the victim, not claiming your actions at all. Yet you sit pointing the finger and involving everyone else.

Damn friend I thought you were better than that; when all the while you were just another scandalous imposter waiting for your moment to throw salt in my wounds.

Self-Discovery

I've discovered me today, finally I've accepted her for whom she is and I'm proud. Allowing her to shine and be true to self, her happiness is also her complete bliss.

I've discovered the paths that needed to be taken for I've never traveled those paths before now I'm happy.

Confidence has prepared me and changed my direction now I can smile for I know what I want out of life.

I've discovered sacrifice and will. Now I know I will give my all to make it no matter what. For only I can shape and mold my future, which will give hope and the riches of education to my blood line and fertilize the seeds of my family to come.

I've discovered hope, for hope is what keeps dreams alive. Hope helps to speak all things into existence. Now I hope, I dream and dream for me and today I experienced my self-discovery.

Shadow

It's a funny thing me. Amazed by how much joy I bring, although stepped on I don't feel a thing, the insane run from me. The spiritualists see a lot in me, thinking my being is of other things.

I'm on the stage while the singer sings, accompanying the band play out their dreams. On the playground with the children laughing, crawling and falling. When you make sudden stops from fear, I too am stalling.

Dancing on the walls; I move to your groove and at your crying hours I'm there to soothe. Never leaving your side, only to you I abide. There with you 'til the end your shadow a.k.a. your best friend.

So Here I Sit

I sit thinking of you; watching the sunshine, enjoying the view wishing I could share the moment with you.

I sit listening to your favorite song; learning the lyrics, drifting deeper into your world. Closing my eyes I visualize you, your body and the way it felt the first and last time you held me.

I sit remembering your smell; thoughts in gulfed as if I were in a forbidden garden, taking in the new and exotic scents of you. Lost again, but this time on a voyage of pure enchantment.

I sit wondering if you feel as strong for me. Wondering if you meant to cast this bewitching spell on me.

I sit dazed with feelings of completion when I think of you. Thinking; if giving the task of writing about you which word or words I'd use. Thinking of you one word comes to mind, so I'd choose love and love every time. If I had to paint a picture of love, it would look just like you. If I had to give love a smell it would smell just like you. If ever to taste love, I wish for it to taste like you. If I could embrace love, it would feel just like you. If I had to give love a voice, it would sound just like you, and if ever asked to define love my definition would simply be you.

So here I sit thinking, watching, listening, remembering, smelling, wondering, feeling and writing. How it could, did, should, would and will feel to be with you. So here I sit wanting you. So here I sit wishing for you. So here I sit waiting on you. So here I sit.

Thank You

You allowed your selfishness to spill out of your mouth again, only caring about how things would affect you and caring the least about how I would feel. Trying to puzzle me you used wicked logic against me, knowing all along that you were the king of games I fell for your game this time but never again. The words that dripped from your lips landed in my mind causing a flood of foolishness, now I'm swimming in my own stupidity, dizzy from the dangerous current you tried to pull me into but I survived and I'm a float, never to be drowned by a man again. I can't blame you completely, because I saw your game coming a mile away. I just wasn't sure when the distance would get this close. Your actions were running a mile a minute and your motive was to leave a lifetime of hurt that would never be fully forgotten. You must've doubted my strength, thinking I was as weak as the other women that came in and out of your life. But I proved you wrong, I'm stronger. I'm all cried out and not another tear will fall for you. I'm even stronger now, and I thank you.

Thoughts of Desperation

You replay in my mind like a classic movie scene. I'm seeing you over and over again. I know your every thought, got all your lines down to a science, yet I'm not convinced. Your cries of love, care and the wanting to be there. Your smile, tears and now here lately your voice is the sound I continue to hear.

Although I try to keep myself away from you, loneliness seems to draw me to you. When you're in my presence old feelings take control, and I give to you my mind, heart, body and my soul. The feel of your touch, your soft caress and the way you allow me to nuzzle close and rest my head on your chest. The way you run your fingertips down my naked spine and your whispers of always being mine. You're funny like that Valentine I've heard so many speak of, and I can't decipher if these are thoughts of loneliness, desperation or love.

Thug Angel

Just another day riding through the hood, I kept checking my rear view making sure I looked good. Hit Market Street; traffic light stopping me and out of nowhere a thug angel appeared blinding me.

Tall, dark, with dredz blowing in the wind. This one I had to have, if not as a lover at least as a friend. Madly sexual in a Rasta thugged out kind of way, I gave him my number and prayed he'd call that day.

Multitudes of attraction with every word that he speaks. Each motion and action makes my body weak. Although he strikes me as being on some ole next type crazy shit. I'm feeling him and I'm willing to abide with it. Advantage; hopefully won't be taking on any part, because with one look this ruffian stole my heart.

Trapped

Trapped in this cubical with posters of motivation, notes to self and quotes to" be all you can be", yet I'm stuck in this job that doesn't match me or my creative ability. Knowing that I have many talents and my goals are obtainable, yet I sit here and the more I sit they begin to seem unreachable.

Trying to stay optimistic, focused and true, but being creative doesn't pay the bills so what does one do?

I'm an artist! I'm not conventional! God gave me these talents and I refuse to let him down or let them go, because my talents are intentional.

Born with a purpose to do great things, I will not allow my mental barricade to trap me from spreading my wings, I will believe in myself and let God do the rest. Releasing all mental restraints I'm no longer creatively oppressed.

Escaping from the chains that held me down for so long I'm finally free, never will I allow anything including myself to trap me again.

Wasteland

I'm a wasteland of former lovers that wanted nothing to do with me. Left without love or want, just the ability to continue to roll with the punches, pain and bruises of lust.

I'm a wasteland filled with used condoms, ejaculation, and children that will never bore, for their daddies will never want them. Like a barrenness I've been left bleak and lifeless.

I'm a wasteland of hopeless promises of true love, emotionless faces, and lying lovers. Not following the teaching of believing nothing that I see; half of what I hear and trusting no one. I continue to get caught up and hurt each and every time. Trying to love and make someone love me by giving of myself too soon, yet I'm never taken seriously and I can't question why for I know the answer is me.

I'm a wasteland of giving them what they want even when their lying, knowing what they really want is sex with no strings, but my mind makes me believe other things.

I'm a wasteland of stupidity, yet I keep being stupid, living in a fairytale world that makes me believe I've got my shit together when in hind sight I need to gather my shit and put it together for real.

I'm a wasteland of blackened hearts that reflect evil grins that laugh at me when my back is turned, although they think I can't hear them I feel them and it burns. Cutting me deep inside, I can't really feel any more for this pain is too familiar. Like Deja vu this is happening over and over again. Trying to numb myself and move on, but the baggage of the past keeps reappearing making its presence known. I revert back to nonsense, yet I know I'm tired of the unthinkable scheme of love. Knowing change is up to me I want to dismiss my dark, damaged and destroyed reputation and once again be that cultivated refined garden I use to be, burying this wasteland that has become of me.

What a Sweet Ride

Tasting the sugar in your kisses I crave you, so I'm left wanting more.

More of your time, the feel of you touch just more of you. When we're not together, I can smell you and visualize your deep dark skin. You're a permanency in my mind like you've always been for many years and that's special to me, because not too many men have left lasting impressions on me like this. You're one of a kind so I choose to call you sweetness, for there's no other word to describe you. Even if I tried to kill my feelings for you they would live on, because my feelings for you will be everlasting.

A few times I thought of letting what we have go completely because I know you have someone and as much as my mind tells my heart this. The more my heart latches onto you. I don't feel like our meeting again was accidental, but something meant to happen. Yet I have to caution myself for the fall.

In love people don't always last forever, but I'm trying to be hopeful. Some days I want to scream about our friendship, yet I silence myself with fear of talking too much and destroying everything.

Not knowing the time line of what we have I guess I'll just have to ride this thing we have until the wheels fall off, or learn to take full control of my emotions . . . But what a sweet ride it is.

About The Author

MarQuetta "Shy Stilletto" Preston

The author was born in Chester, Pennsylvania and raised in the quiet city of New Castle, Delaware. A poet, abstract artist, freelance make-up artist and fashion blogger. MarQuetta considers herself a lover of all things creative. If she isn't spending time with her friends and family, you can almost always bet that she is creating something artistic, Ambigu ous Interpretations... Step into my world is MarQuetta's first book of poetry.

WARE RESOURCES AND PUBLISHING

WE ARE AN ALL IN ONE,

ONE STOP PUBLISHING COMPANY!!!!

W.R.P. is a modest but skillful and knowledgeable Christian Publishing Company. We specialize in getting authors into print. We embrace and guide each author like a member of our family. We treat you fairly and recognize the importance of building a lasting relationship with you as an author. Join us in the walk to promote prosperity along with the message of encouragement and peace. Be one of the authors we transform and prepare for the world of information and books.

FEEL FREE TO CONTACT US @

www.wareresources.com 1-888-469-4850 EXT. 2

http://www.facebook.com/pages/Ware-Resources-and-Publishing

Ware Resources and Publishing

You Start and Finish With Us!

www.ingramcontent.com/pod-product-compliance
Lightning Source LLC
Chambersburg PA
CBHW062152100526
44589CB00014B/1804